GOD'S
DAD JOKES

PUNNY HUMOR OF BIBLICAL PROPORTIONS

I0458623

Recorded by S. S. Coulter
Illustrated by Fernando Medina

These are God's jokes; we just wrote them down.

ISBN: 978-1-959568-14-8
SSCoulter.com

In January 2025, I was in prayer when I felt God move me to write a joke book. A joke book? I had seen many Dad Joke Books for sale, and I guess it was time for the Heavenly Father to join in on the fun! From that moment, I was inundated with God's Dad Jokes. I would be in my prayer closet laughing as more and more jokes came. I'd watch TV and have to write them down. I'd be reading my Bible ... the jokes were everywhere! In just two short, joy-filled weeks, I had written down over 100 jokes!

I still have my childhood Bible. It has a picture of Jesus smiling on it; a picture that captured my heart when I was a little girl. Although the Jesus I would see at church services was usually somber and serious, the Jesus I had in my heart was happy and, yes, even FUNNY! God is infinite, and He made each of us in His image, uniquely created to reveal different parts of His Character to one another. I hope this book gives you a little glimpse into the part of Jesus who smiles, laughs, and loves to tell a good "bad dad" joke.

May God shine His smiling face upon your laughter.

S. S. Coulter

DEAR: ....
....
....
....
....
....
....
....

FROM: ....

DRUM ROLL PLEASE...

WHY DOESN'T GOD TALK IN THE PAST TENSE?

BECAUSE HE'S THE GREAT I AM.

Exodus 3:14

Did God sleep on the 7th day?
No, He was just resting His eyes.

Genesis 2:2

WHAT ARE JESUS'S FAVORITE BUGS?
LIGHTNING BUGS

Matthew 5:14-16

Why doesn't Eve like when Adam laughs too hard?

It hurts his ribs.

Genesis 2:21-22

What did Elizabeth say when John leaped in her womb?
That ain't gas!

———

Luke 1:44

WHAT DID THE DONKEY SAY TO BALAAM?

DON'T BE SUCH A ... ME.

Numbers 22:28

What did the angels say to the women at the tomb on Sunday?

Jesus isn't here. He's not much of a mourning person.

Luke 24:1-6

WHAT IS JESUS'S FAVORITE LUNCH?
WONDER BREAD WITH MIRACLE WHIP.

Acts 2:22

Jesus's teaching that He's the bread of life isn't on a knead to know basis.

John 6:35

What was the first animal Adam named?
Bob

———

Genesis 2:19-20

THE LADDER THAT JACOB SAW WAS REALLY UP TO SOMETHING.

Genesis 28:12-13

WHY WERE THE APOSTLES SO THIRSTY IN THE UPPER ROOM?

THEY HAD TONGUES OF FIRE.

Acts 2:3

WHAT'S JESUS'S FAVORITE SOAP BRAND?
DOVE

———

Luke 3:22

WHAT DID THE 3 KINGS SAY TO JESUS?

WE HAVE GOLD AND MYRRH, AND FRANK SENT THIS.

Matthew 2:11

WHEN PEOPLE SAY HEAVEN ISN'T THE BEST, YOU NEED TO TELL THEM THAT IT'S REALLY UP THERE.

Mark 16:15

Why were there so many donkeys in the Bible?

It's hard to speak the Word when you're hoarse.

Donkeys are portrayed in the Bible as symbols of peace, humility, and service.

WHY WERE SO MANY WOMEN NAMED MARY IN THE BIBLE?

THE MORE, THE MARY-ER.

There were many Marys in the Bible: Mary the mother of Jesus, Mary Magdalene, Mary of Bethany, Mary the mother of James and Joseph, Mary the mother of John Mark, and Mary who Paul asked the church at Rome to greet.

WHAT IS THE HOLIEST CHEESE?
SWISS CHEESE

This joke is too cheesy to have a Bible reference.

WHAT DO YOU CALL AN ANGEL WORKING WITH MOSES?

THE HOST WITH THE MOSES.

Exodus 3:2

What did Elijah say to the false prophets?

It's time to get this Baal rolling.

---

1 Kings 18:16-40

What was Paul's favorite letter to write?

He was fond of Rs, but Qs were fun to write too...

The apostle Paul wrote letters to churches in Rome, Corinth, Galatia, Ephesus, Philippi, Colossae, and Thessalonica.

WHY DID GOD SAVE JONAH?
HE KEPT WHALING FOR HELP.

Jonah 2

How did Eve convince Adam to bite the apple?

Honey, it's crisp!

Genesis 3:6

WHY WERE JEZEBEL AND AHAB IN CAHOOTS?

THEY THOUGHT THEY COULD SPLIT THE PROPHET.

---

1 Kings 19:1-2.

Jesus and Lazarus were great friends who could always count on each other to rise to the occasion.

John 11:38-44, Matthew 28:6, Luke 24:6

Why didn't the apostles have goatees?

Beards were much more sheepish.

Matthew 25:32

Why does Jesus's signature always have to be first?

His is the name above all names.

———

Philippians 2:9-11

Why did the chicken cross the road?
Because Moses wasn't there to part the sea.

Exodus 14:21

Why do women want a waistline like the path to Heaven?

Because it's narrow.

Matthew 7:14

If you ever need help with your boat, I Noah guy.

Genesis 6:13-22

Why didn't Cain please God?

It's because he wasn't willing, not because he wasn't Abel.

———

Genesis 4:4-7

HOW DID JESUS ASSIST THE MAN IN THE SYNAGOGUE?

HE GAVE HIM A HAND.

Matthew 12:13

WHOEVER SAID YOU CAN'T SQUEEZE WATER FROM A STONE NEVER TALKED TO MOSES!

Exodus 17:6

Why did Jesus get kicked off the swim team?

He kept walking on the water.

Matthew 14:25-27

What was Miriam and the women's favorite song to sing?
It's Raining Man-na.

Exodus 15:20, Exodus 16:4

Why did the people listen so intently to Jesus?

They were all heirs.

Romans 8:17

WHOEVER STOLE MY BIBLE, I WILL FIND YOU. YOU HAVE MY WORD.

John 1:1

WHEN MOSES HAD A HEADACHE, GOD TOLD HIM TO TAKE TWO TABLETS AND CALL HIM IN THE MORNING.

Exodus 31:18

Did you hear about the meat God sent into the desert?

It apparently was some quail-ity stuff!

Exodus 16:13

What did Peter say to the guard?
Lend me your ear.

John 18:10

Why did Paul send letters?
Because there wasn't any email.

The Epistles

WHAT DID THE MAN SAY TO JESUS WHEN HE WAS LOWERED THROUGH THE ROOF?

SORRY TO DROP IN ON YOU ...

Mark 2:3-4

Sodom and Gomorrah really went down in flames.

Genesis 19:24-25

I WANT TO TELL MORE JOKES ABOUT SODOM AND GOMORRAH, BUT THERE'S NOTHING THERE.

Genesis 19:24-25

Why is "arm day" Jesus's main workout day?

The government is upon His shoulders.

Isaiah 9:6

WHAT DID JOHN THE BAPTIST SAY TO THE CAMEL?
NICE OUTFIT.

Matthew 3:4

Elijah was a huge fan of the food he had by the river. He was always raven about it.

---

1 Kings 17:4-6

WHEN MOSES'S MOM PUT HIM IN THE BASKET, SHE WAS REALLY IN DE-NILE.

Exodus 2:3

WHY DID THE ANIMALS COME 2X2?
BECAUSE NOAH HAD USED UP ALL THE 2X4S.

Genesis 6:20

The Tower of Babel was wrong on so many levels.

Genesis 11:1-9

Fathers and sons can relate to Abraham and Isaac's relationship. Sometimes taking a trip together may seem burdensome, but once it's done, they realize it wasn't a sacrifice after all.

Genesis 22:1-13

WHEN SOME DISCIPLES TURNED AWAY FROM JESUS AFTER HE TOLD THEM HE WAS THE BREAD OF LIFE, HE REMAINED CALM AND DIDN'T TURN ALL SOURDOUGH ABOUT IT.

John 6:48-69

What lake did the pigs run into after Jesus cast demons into them?

The Bay of Pigs.

———

Matthew 8:32, Luke 8:33

WHY DIDN'T THE APOSTLES NEED FLASHLIGHTS?

THE WORD WAS A LAMP TO THEIR FEET.

Psalm 119:105

WHAT DID LOT SAY TO HIS WIFE?
DON'T BE SO SALTY.

Genesis 19:26

IF JESUS HAD A HOTEL, IT WOULDN'T MAKE ANY MONEY. PEOPLE WHO'D STAY THERE WOULD SIMPLY RISE, TAKE UP THEIR BED, AND GO HOME.

———

John 5:8

God, what rhymes with Nebuchadnezzar?
No, it doesn't.

———

King Nebuchadnezzar is mentioned in the Bible in the books of 2 Kings, 2 Chronicles, Jeremiah, Ezekiel, and Daniel. He is mentioned by name over 80 times.

WHY DID THE EGGS BREAK UP?
BECAUSE THEY WERE UNEQUALLY YOKED.

2 Corinthians 6:14

WHEN THE ISRAELITES LIVED 40 YEARS IN THE DESERT, IT WAS REALLY IN TENTS.

———

Exodus 19:2, Numbers 14:34

WHAT IS A MATHEMATICIAN'S FAVORITE BOOK OF THE BIBLE?

NUMBERS

———

Numbers is the fourth book of the Bible.

Why didn't Zacharia speak to Elizabeth for so long?

It was a mute point.

Luke 1:20-22

What's Jesus's favorite spice blend?
Shadrach, Meshach, and oregano.

Daniel 3:16-30

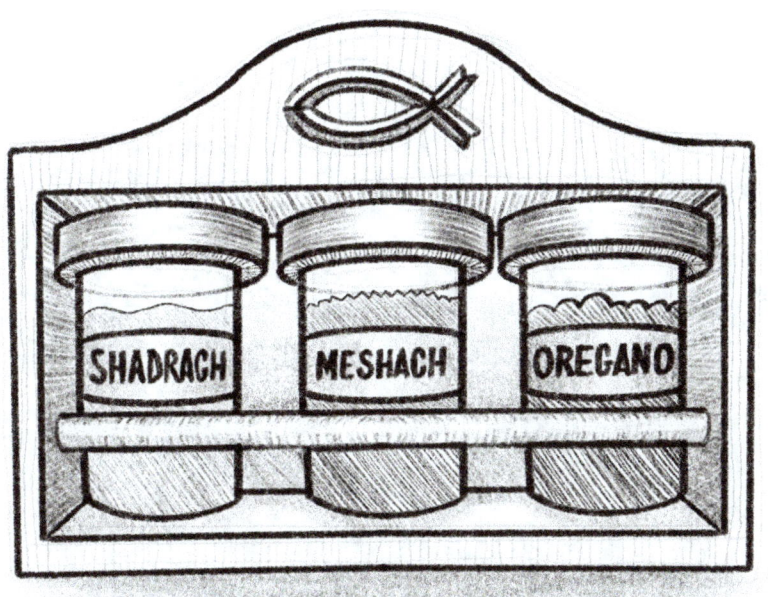

WHAT IS THE MOST BIBLICAL MAKEUP?
A FIRM FOUNDATION

2 Timothy 2:19

What was the size of the water bin Jesus used?

At least 24 feet.

John 13:4-5

You know what they said when Moses went up Mount Sinai?

He was getting over the hill.

———

Exodus 19

Why did Jesus like to wear sandals?
They had good soles.

Matthew 3:11

Why did the priests burn incense?
Because God didn't ask them to burn in dollars.

Exodus 30:7

What did the widow say to Elisha?
This is all going to pot.

2 Kings 4:1-7

What's another name for Chariots of Fire?
Holy Smokes

---

2 Kings 2:11

Believe me! David wrestled a bear! That's no lion, man.

1 Samuel 17:34–37

WHAT'S JESUS'S FAVORITE KIND OF SHOP?
A LAMP STAND

Exodus 25:31

The shepherds who encountered the angels when Jesus was born were so happy they were out working that night. They just kept saying, "Thank goodness we herd!"

Luke 2:8-14

What do angels and the ocean have in common?

They bring good tidings.

Luke 2:10

What room does Daniel try to avoid?
The den

Daniel 6

Jesus may only order water at a bar, but He gives a lot of tips.

John 2:1-11

What is David's favorite idiom?
Kill one giant with one stone.

---

1 Samuel 17:49

Holy Spirit got your tongue?

Acts 2:4

Did you hear the one about Samson and Delilah?

It was a hairy situation.

Judges 16:19

Why did Jesus so quickly tell the sick man at the Pool of Bethesda to "Get up! Pick up your bed and walk"?

He didn't want him to sleep on it.

_____

John 5:1-9

You know when Peter first joined Jesus ... he really felt like a fisherman out of water.

Luke 5:1-11

WHY WERE DENTISTS RELUCTANT TO PULL TEETH BEFORE JESUS'S TIME?

BEFORE JESUS, IT WAS A TOOTH FOR A TOOTH.

Matthew 5:38-42

WHAT HAPPENED WHEN THE APOSTLES TAUGHT THE GOSPEL?

THEY WERE CONSTANTLY ON THE LAMB.

Acts 5:17-42

You think David had a lot of wives ... at least he wasn't Solo-man.

---

1 Kings 11:3

3 MEN WALKED INTO A FIRE ... IT WAS HOT, BUT IT WAS NO MATCH FOR THE SON.

Daniel 3:16-30

Some say John the Baptist was a little nervous when he baptized Jesus; he had locusts in his stomach.

Matthew 3:4

WHAT IS JESUS'S FAVORITE TYPE OF POPCORN?
LIGHT AND SALTY

Matthew 5:13-16

LIGHT & SALTY

What is Jesus's favorite nursery rhyme?
Mary Had a Little Lamb

John 1:29

WHAT WAS THE MOST POPULAR DRINK IN THE BIBLE?

WATER AND WINE ARE MENTIONED A LOT, BUT MOST EVENTS WENT FOR-TEA.

The number 40 appears in the Bible 159 times across both the Old and New Testaments. For example, Moses, Elijah, and Jesus each fasted for 40 days and nights; the Israelites wandered the desert for 40 years; God flooded the earth for 40 days and nights; Saul, David, and Solomon reigned for 40 years; Goliath taunted Isreal for 40 days before David defeated him, and so much more...

What is Jesus's favorite Mexican food?
Holy mole

If Mexican food was around in Biblical times, Jesus probably would have also liked Tacos al Pastor ...

KNOCK, KNOCK.
WHO'S THERE?
ORANGE.
ORANGE WHO?
ORANGE YOU GLAD I WASHED MY FEET?

———

A basic act of hospitality in Biblical times was to wash one's feet before entering a house because wearing sandals caused feet to become very dirty.

SOMETIMES IF JESUS LOOKED FRUSTRATED, HIS DISCIPLES WOULD LOOK AT HIM AND SIMPLY SAY, "YOU ROCK."

Isaiah 26:4.

SOME PEOPLE DON'T BELIEVE IN THE PROMISED LAND OF THE OLD TESTAMENT, BUT I CAN TELL YOU, IS-RAEL.

In the Old Testament, Israel is referred to as the Promised Land in Genesis, Exodus, Joshua, and other books. The Promised Land is the land God promised to Abraham and his descendants.

WHAT IS THE REAL MEANING OF REVELATION?
GOD ONLY KNOWS.

Revelation 22:18-21

Why did the Israelites wander in the desert for so long?
They didn't follow the signs.

Joshua 5:6

You know what they say about fasting ... it's better than slowing.

WHAT'S THE BEST MEAL AFTER A LONG FAST?
BREAK-FAST

Biblical fasting is a spiritual practice of voluntarily abstaining from food for a set period of time and for a specific purpose. It's a way to connect with God, seek guidance, and demonstrate humility.

HOLY SPIRIT REALLY LIKES CLEAN SHEETS. YOU WOULD TOO IF YOU WERE THE COMFORTER.

Remember that Holy Spirit likes clean sheets?

You would too if you were the Holy Ghost.

———

John 14:16. The Holy Spirit of God, the third Person of the Trinity, is the Spirit of God Himself who is ready to teach, guide, and comfort just as Jesus promised He would.

How do you get part of God's inheritance?

You have to be in His will.

———

1 John 5:14-15

GOD MAY DRESS THE LILIES WITH BEAUTY AND SPLENDOR, BUT HIS FAVORITE FLOWER IS THE SON-FLOWER.

Matthew 6:28-30

When Jesus reviewed the Gospels, He started with John. He sat on a Matt, Luked it over, and Marked it up.

The Gospels are Matthew, Mark, Luke, and John.

Why were Elisha's bones so alarming?
They sure woke that guy up!

2 Kings 13:20-21

WHEN IT WAS TIME TO FEED THE MULTITUDES, JESUS TOLD THE DISCIPLES THEY HAD TO STOP LOAF-ING AROUND AND BE MORE E-FISH-IENT.

Mark 6:35-44, Mark 8:1-9

WHAT MUSICAL INSTRUMENT WERE MANY OF THE APOSTLES FOND OF?

CAST-A-NETS

The apostles Peter, Andrew, James, John, and Philip were all fishermen.

What did the Jews say to the angel of death?

We'll take a Pass-Over here.

Exodus 12:23

What's Jesus's favorite Karate move?
The lamb chop

John 1:29

WHEN IT'S RAINING CATS AND DOGS, I THINK OF EGYPT AND THANK GOD IT'S NOT GNATS AND FROGS!

Exodus 8:1-19

AND THAT'S ALL HE WROTE ... FOR NOW.

———

Give thanks to the LORD, for He is good;
His love endures forever.
—
Psalm 107:1

A joyful heart is good medicine.
—
Proverbs 17:22

In Your presence is fullness of joy.
—
Psalm 16:11